The Unexplained

UFOs

By

John Duncan

GARETH STEVENS
GS
PUBLISHING
A Member of the WRC Media Family of Companies

Please visit our web site at: www.garethstevens.com
For a free color catalog describing Gareth Stevens Publishing's
list of high-quality books and multimedia programs,
call 1-800-542-2595 or 1-800-387-3178 (Canada).
Gareth Stevens Publishing's Fax: (414) 332-3567.

Library of Congress Cataloging-in-Publication Data

Duncan, John, 1952–
    UFOs / John Duncan. — North American ed.
       p. cm. — (The unexplained)
    Includes bibliographical references and index.
    ISBN 0-8368-6268-6 (lib. bdg.)
    1. Unidentified flying objects—Juvenile literature.
    2. Human-alien encounters—Juvenile literature. I. Title.
    II. Series.
  TL789.2D86   2006
  001.942—dc22   2005054078

This North American edition first published in 2006 by
Gareth Stevens Publishing
A Member of the WRC Media Family of Companies
330 West Olive Street, Suite 100
Milwaukee, WI 53212 USA

This U.S. edition copyright © 2006 by Gareth Stevens, Inc. Original
edition copyright © 2003 ticktock Entertainment Ltd. First published
in Great Britain in 2003by ticktock Publishib Ltd., Unit 2, Orchard
Business Centre, North Farm Road, Tunbridge Wells, Kent, TN2 3XF.

Gareth Stevens editor: Monica Rausch
Gareth Stevens art direction: Tammy West

Picture Credits: t = top, b = bottom, c = center, l = left, r= right,
OFC = outside front cover, OBC = outside back cover, IFC = inside
front cover
Ann Ronan@Image Select; 4tl, 28bl, 29cr. AKG; 5tr, 4/5b, 6b, 6c, 8/9b,
8/9c, 9cr, 9tr, 10cl, 13bc, 12/13c, 15r, 14tl, 117br, 16tr, 18/19(main pic),
19cl, 19tl & 34, 23c, 24c, 24cr, 25, 26tl, 31c. CFCL; 22l. Corbis; 11tr,
OBC & 12c, 15cl, 23tr. Et archive; 22/23tc, 28/29t. Fortean Picture
Library; 4/5c, 13tr, 13/14c, 16/17c, 18tl, 20c, 20b, 26tl & OFC, 26/27bc,
27c, 27, 31tr, 31bc, 33b. Images CWP; 12/13t, 17tr, 28tl. The Kobal
collection; 8tl, 23bl & IFC, 24tl, 23b. Mary Evans; 26/27c. Planet Earth
Pictures; 10tl, 10/11br, 19r, 28/29c, 33tc. Rex features; 21tl, 30/31c, 30,
30tr, 32bc. Science Photo Library; 32tl. Spectrum; 4bl. Telegraph
Colour Library; OFC, 6/7r, 6tl, 10c, 10/11tc, 20tl,
20(main pic), 32cr, 32/33t. Werner Foreman; 14b.

Every effort has been made to trace the copyright holders and we apologize in
advance for any unintentional omissions. We would be pleased to insert the
appropriate acknowledgement in any subsequent edition of this publication.

Printed in the United States of America

1 2 3 4 5 6 7 8 9 10 09 08 07 06

CONTENTS

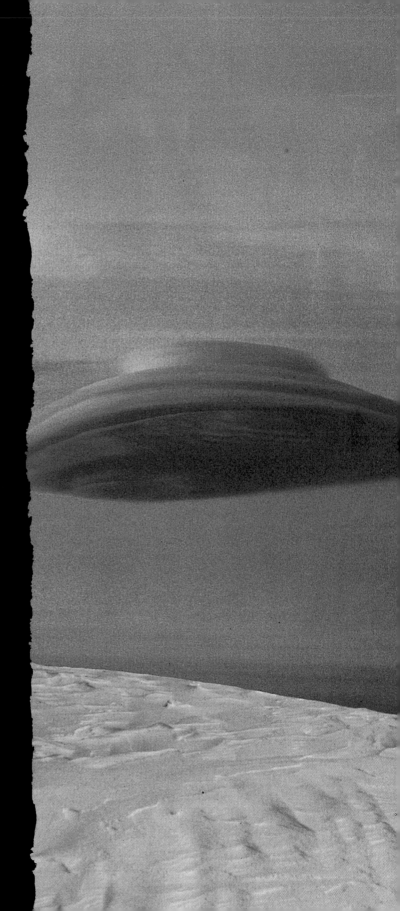

ARE ALIENS LANDING?

hroughout history, humans have
eported seeing strange objects in
he sky. Could these unidentified flying
bjects (UFOs) be natural phenomena,
r are they signs that other life forms
xist far out in space?

ANCIENT UFOS

ALIEN FOOTPRINT

This fossilized footprint (above) from East Africa was believed to have been made by a prehistoric, two-footed mammal that was an ancestor to humans. Some UFOlogists, however, claim the print predates *Homo erectus*, the ancestor of modern humans; they believe it was made by an alien.

Throughout history, people have recorded seeing strange phenomena in the sky. In the Bible, the prophet Ezekiel wrote, "In the thirtieth year, in the fourth month, on the fifth day, by the river Chebar, I saw something that looked like burning coals of fire." Ezekiel described how he saw wheels in the sky gleaming like a jewel, "being as it were a wheel within a wheel." Ezekiel interpreted his experience as a vision of God. Today, some UFOlogists, or people who study unidentified flying objects (UFOs), would suggest Ezekiel's vision was one of the first recorded sightings of a UFO.

ANCIENT ABDUCTIONS

In Celtic legends, fairies (left) were said to steal babies from their cots and replace them with fairy infants. To keep babies safe, medieval peasants hung a knife over the cradle. Were these so-called fairies actually aliens—possibly taking human babies to study them?

What do YOU think ?

William Occam, a medieval philosopher, noted that simple, common-sense explanations for mysteries are usually right; we do not need to invent new, weird theories to explain odd events. Some people, for example, believe that most of the phenomena reported on these two pages have perfectly reasonable explanations— and have nothing to do with alien visits.

PREHISTORIC RECORDS

These prehistoric rock drawings (above) from Peru seem to show astronauts wearing space helmets. Cave paintings in other locations have shown disks in the sky. The Bible notes that at one time "the sons of God" came down and took human wives (Book of Genesis). Could the drawings and the biblical verse possibly be referring to alien visits?

A DESERT MYSTERY

Over one thousand years ago in Nazca, Peru, thousands of stones were arranged to make vast lines and huge figures in the desert. These stone arrangements still remain. The images they make, including these "aliens" (above), are clearly visible from the air, but when a person is standing on the ground, the figures are not noticeable since they are too large to see as a whole. In 1969, the writer Erich von Däniken suggested that these Nazca forms were made to be visible to aliens flying overhead in spaceships. He also suggested that these "ancient astronauts" interfered with human genes and affected how humans developed technology. He believes they shaped human history.

DIFFERENT VISIONS

Throughout history, UFOs seem to appear to people in whatever form they expect to see them. According to the Bible, the prophet Elijah was carried away by a chariot of fire (right). In 1897, Americans saw "airships" floating in the sky. In the 1950s, people reported seeing metal spaceships.

ELIJAH TRANSLATED INTO HEAVEN

Elisha saw it, and he cried My father, my father, the Chariot of Israel, and he saw him no more.
II Kings, ch. II. ver. II.

Pub. by Hogg & Cᵒ Paternoster row.

Famous Sightings in History

C. 1450 B.C., Egypt
Pharaoh Thutmose III reports seeing "circles of fire" in the sky.

322 B.C., Lebanon
Shining silver shields fly over a city being attacked by Alexander the Great. The shields are said to have fired beams of light at the city's defenses, destroying the city walls.

A.D. 840, France
The Archbishop of Lyons stops people from killing two creatures who came to Earth in a "cloud ship."

1211, Ireland
The people of Cloera try to catch creatures whose "airship" supposedly caught on their church roof.

1271, Japan
The execution of a Buddhist monk is called off when a bright object is seen hanging in the sky above the execution site.

1492, Atlantic Ocean
A sailor on one of Christopher Columbus's ships, the *Santa Maria*, reports seeing a glittering object in the sky.

1639, Massachusetts
James Everell is fishing with friends when a bright light hovers over them and moves their boat upstream.

1752, Sweden
Farmers claim to see a large, shining cylinder in the sky "give birth" to smaller balls of light.

1762, Switzerland
In different towns, two astronomers independently record seeing a "spindle-shaped" aircraft move across the face of the Sun.

1819, Massachusetts
Professor Rufus Graves sees a fireball crash into the yard of his friend Erastus Dewey. They reportedly find UFO wreckage and, inside it, a foul-smelling pulpy substance.

1820, United States
Mormon leader Joseph Smith reports seeing a UFO and says he talked with its occupants.

1861, Chile
Peasants claim to see a metal bird with shining eyes and sharp scales.

1868, England
Astronomers at the Radcliffe Observatory at Oxford University reportedly track a UFO for four minutes.

1887, Banjos, Spain
Villagers find two "children" in a cave. According to the villagers, their clothes are strange, they speak no known language, and their skin is green.

SIGHTINGS

Every year, over a thousand UFOs are sighted. Many people who sight UFOs ask to remain anonymous because they are afraid other people might think they are crazy. Others, however, including several famous people, have openly reported seeing UFOs. In 1963, Gordon Cooper, a U.S. astronaut, claimed to have seen a glowing green object on his space flight. This same object also appeared on Australian radar. In 1965, space-walkers Ed White and James McDivitt reported seeing a metallic UFO with "arms" sticking out in all directions. Former U.S. president Jimmy Carter reported that he once watched a UFO while attending a dinner party, and former U.S. president Ronald Reagan announced during a White House meeting that he had once seen a UFO from the window of his plane.

What do YOU think

In the 1960s, the U.S. Air Force's Project Blue Book studied 13,000 UFO sightings. The project found that only about 2 percent of the UFOs actually were unidentifiable. Most UFOs are natural phenomena and can be identified or explained. Possible identities for UFOs include:

- Aircraft and satellites
- Weather balloons
- Jupiter and other planets, when they are unusually bright Autokinesis, a visual illusion, also can make them appear to move.
- Meteors
- Signs of a coming earthquake. Canadian scientists have found that stress on rocks just before an earthquake can produce strong electrical fields and strange lights.
- Vitreous floaters, or matter moving inside a person's eye
- The effects of wishful thinking, hysteria, or mental or emotional disturbances

Some people believe UFO sightings that are still unexplained are likely to be either secret military experiments or natural phenomena we do not yet fully understand.

ALIEN WARFARE

This woodcut (right) was made in 1561 and apparently records a frightening event in Germany. Black and red balls of light seem to battle each other in the sky. Some UFOlogists suggest that two alien species were fighting for control of Earth.

WHITE LIGHT

Jeremy Johnson took this photograph (left) of a UFO in England in 1992. He said at first he thought he had missed his chance to capture it on film because the white object vanished as soon as he pointed the camera at it.

THE AIRSHIP PHENOMENON

In 1897, many people in the United States saw shining, cigar-shaped "airships." This illustration (right) was drawn for a newspaper at the time. Many people believed they were not seeing a human-made airship, even though a man named E. J. Pennington said the ship belonged to him.

FLATTENED FOREST

In 1908, an explosion in Siberia, Russia, flattened trees for miles around (opposite). Investigators found no crater from the impact of a meteor and no meteor fragments. According to some modern theories, a comet or a small black hole may have caused the explosion. Local people, however, reported seeing an elliptical fireball rise up from the ground. They also later suffered an illness that resembled radiation sickness. UFOlogists suggest the phenomenon was an exploding spaceship.

UFOLOGY IS BORN

Kenneth Arnold made perhaps one of the most influential UFO sightings. In June 1947, Arnold reportedly saw nine V-shaped UFOs (above). He told a newspaper reporter they moved at speeds of over 1,000 miles (1,600 kilometers) per hour and traveled "like a saucer would if you skipped it across the water." The reporter's news article on Arnold's "Flying Saucers" captured the public's imagination. *Fate Magazine*, the first of many publications about UFOs, was published a year later.

FOO FIGHTERS

During World War II, many British and U.S. pilots reported seeing small, shining disks, which they called "foo fighters," following their planes and causing the planes' engines to short out. One UFOlogist thought these disks were remote-controlled alien probes. This World War II photograph (above) appears to show clearly these mysterious disks in the sky.

THE ROSWELL INCIDENT

This artist's reconstruction of the Roswell incident (above) shows a UFO being struck by lightning during the storm on July 4, 1

THE TRUTH IS OUT THERE

On July 8, 1947, Grady Barnett, a local engineer, added to the Roswell mystery when he and a team of archaeologists claimed to have found a crashed, disk-shaped UFO and the bodies of four aliens—small, gray humanoids with large heads. The U.S. Air Force quickly removed the bodies and the wreckage (above). Since then, people have believed the U.S. government is hiding evidence of the crash. Even a U.S. Senate investigation in 1994 failed to convince UFO enthusiasts that the U.S. government does *not* still have the wreckage along with the alien bodies. The idea of a secret, crashed UFO—and of what we might learn by "back-engineering" alien spacecraft—is so attractive that the belief in it is hard to wipe out.

THE MOST FAMOUS UFO

On July 4, 1947, a lightning storm struck the town of Roswell, New Mexico. Sitting in his farmhouse, rancher William "Mac" Brazel thought he heard an explosion above the sounds of the storm. The next day, when Brazel rode out to check on his sheep, he discovered the wreckage of material that was "like nothing made on Earth." He said it crumpled like foil but slowly straightened itself out again and was impervious to blows from a sledgehammer. Brazel reported it to local U.S. Air Force officials, but for mysterious reasons he was quickly arrested and held in custody until the wreckage was retrieved. His find has since become one of the best-known and longest-standing UFO stories.

CAPTURED!

Soon after the story of Kenneth Arnold's "flying saucers" in June 1947, the U.S. Air Force recorded almost a thousand UFO sightings from all over the United States, including reports of downed spacecraft. On July 8, 1947, the press was told that a flying disk was recovered in Roswell. Immediately, the *Roswell Daily Record* reported that the Roswell wreckage was actually a crashed UFO out of which four aliens had been retrieved.

ALIEN AUTOPSY

In 1996, businessman Ray Santilli released a film that he claimed showed autopsies being done in 1947 on alien bodies from the Roswell crash. The film, however, appeared to be faked; it looked like a bad horror movie, and the aliens looked nothing like those supposedly found in the Roswell crash. A modern phone also was clearly visible in the background. UFO enthusiasts, however, were convinced by the film's "evidence." This photo (right) from the Roswell International UFO Museum shows a replica of the alien body from the film's "autopsy."

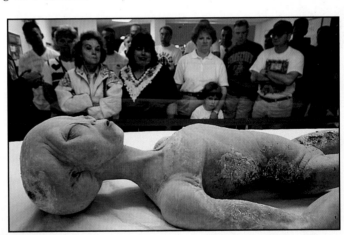

BALLOON WRECKAGE

On July 8, 1947, the U.S. Air Force held two press conferences. At one conference, a polite and very believable young warrant officer (left) showed the press foil debris from a weather balloon that he said was from the Roswell wreckage. When asked if it was the remains of a flying saucer, the young man laughed. Many people, however, thought the officer's explanation was a lie. They believed the U.S. government was keeping something a secret. That same month, a number of U.S. Air Force flights delivered cargo from Roswell to the top-secret Wright-Patterson Air Force base in Ohio. For some people, what the planes were carrying has never been satisfactorily explained.

CLOSE ENCOUNTERS

During the 1950s and 1960s, thousands of UFO sightings were reported, but UFOlogists had no way to analyze or categorize them until Dr. J. Allen Hynek developed a method in 1972. In his book *The UFO Experience*, Dr. Hynek became the first UFOlogist to categorize UFO events and divide them into different types of close encounters. UFOlogists have since classified all UFO events according to his categories, from close encounters of the first kind to close encounters of the fifth kind. Many UFOlogists also give encounter experiences a "strangeness rating" according to how typical they are compared to other similar reported events.

CE2: PROJECT HESSDALEN, NORWAY

From 1981 to 1985, Norwegian scientists (below) studied lights that appeared over Hessdalen, Norway. The lights reportedly moved and seemed to respond to the actions of the observers.

CLOSE ENCOUNTER (CE) CATEGORIES

CE1: Sighting a UFO only
CE2: Finding some physical evidence left by a UFO or alien
CE3: Sighting alien(s)
CE4: Being abducted by aliens
CE5: Humans and aliens meet and interact.
CE6: An animal or human dies during a meeting with aliens.

HESSDALEN LIGHTS

Hessdalen researchers photographed the lights (below) and used radar, seismographs, infrared viewers, spectrum analyzers, and Geiger counters to see if the lights were leaving any physical evidence of their presence.

CLOSE ENCOUNTERS OF THE THIRD KIND

Steven Spielberg's 1977 movie *Close Encounters of the Third Kind* (above) was based on UFOlogist J. Allen Hynek's book, *The UFO Experience* (1972). In the movie, a series of UFO encounters gradually builds up to a friendly meeting between aliens and humans—a CE5. Some people say that the U.S. government asked Spielberg to make the film to calm public fears about UFOs.

A CE1: THE LUBBOCK LIGHTS

In 1951, the people of Lubbock, Texas, reported a V-shaped formation of lights passing overhead at night (above). The lights were said to be traveling at about 400 miles (644 km) per hour. A nearby radar station also recorded an "unknown" object. According to official explanations of the phenomenon, the lights could have been a flight of geese reflected by the street lights or an experimental jet bomber that was tested in the area.

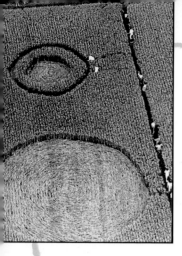

CATTLE MUTILATIONS, CROP CIRCLES, AND OTHER CE2s

CROP CIRCLES

In the 1980s, crop circles began to appear all over the world, especially in Great Britain and Japan (above). UFOlogists suggested they were made by landing spacecraft. The circles received a great deal of publicity.

A close encounter of the second kind is when a UFO leaves some physical evidence of its presence. In one famous example, a farmer from Trans-en-Provence, France, reported in 1981 that an object had landed in his garden. Government investigators found the garden's soil had been heated to 1,112° Fahrenheit (600° Celsius). One scientist suggested the heat had been produced by a strong electromagnetic field. In 1965, however, another farmer, M. Masse, had made a similar report. He claimed a spaceship had landed in his lavender field in Valensole—about 30 miles (48 km) from Trans-en-Provence.

A CE2 OF A DIFFERENT KIND

Stephen Michalak, an amateur geologist, claims to have seen a spaceship near Winnipeg, Canada, in 1967. Apparently, when the craft flew away the heat was so intense that his clothes were set on fire. Later, the pattern of a grille appeared to be burned onto Michalak's chest (left). Some skeptics claimed Michalak had burned himself. Scientists, however, found evidence of radioactivity and extreme heat at the landing site.

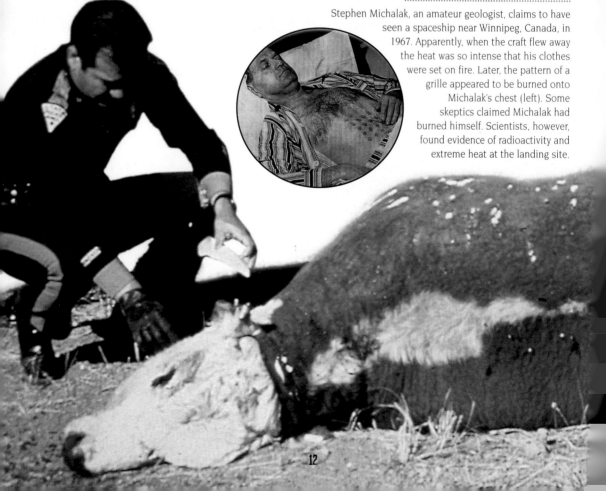

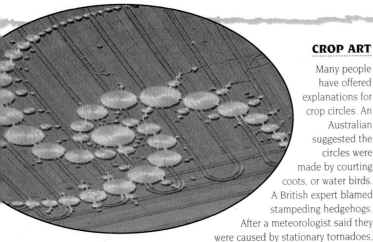

CROP ART

Many people have offered explanations for crop circles. An Australian suggested the circles were made by courting coots, or water birds. A British expert blamed stampeding hedgehogs. After a meteorologist said they were caused by stationary tornadoes, elaborate crop patterns started to appear that could not possibly have been made by the weather. This beautiful example (above) appeared in Wiltshire, England. In 1991, however, two retired artists showed how they had faked many crop patterns in Britain. Strangely, many hoaxers have reported seeing UFOs while they were working on the crop patterns.

HOW DID SNIPPY DIE?

In 1967, a horse called Snippy (left), or, in some accounts, Lady, was found dead on a ranch in Colorado. Her head had been skinned and her internal organs had been removed. No blood was found on the ground, and her body had circular exhaust marks all around it. Similar cases have been reported all over the world. A large number of these horse mutilations occurred in England in the 1980s.

What do YOU think

Why would aliens fly 2,000 light-years to make shapes in fields, and why would such technologically sophisticated beings mutilate thousands of animals to take organs for their studies? These stories are so unbelievable that many people do not think the phenomena are the work of alien visitors. The real danger is that, swamped by the thousands of hoaxers, scientists may miss the one witness who may have experienced a real CE2.

CATTLE MUTILATION

Investigators have recorded hundreds of reports of cattle mutilations like the one shown here in New Mexico (below). Some people suggest a religious group may have mutilated the animals as part of a ritual sacrifice. Investigators, however, have found that the cuts seemed to be made by unknown instruments. The blood in the flesh on either side of the cuts apparently had been cooked at a temperature of about 302° F (150° C), but the actual cells around the cuts were not damaged. An instrument that can do this has yet to be developed.

Aboard a Flying Saucer

by TRUMAN BETHURUM

Non-Fiction—A True Account of Factual Experience

BETHURUM MAKES CONTACT

Truman Bethurum (right) was a road construction worker who, in 1954, claimed to have met aliens in the California desert near Las Vegas. The aliens reportedly had olive green skin and dark hair. They came from Clarion, a planet obscured from Earth by the Moon. Clarion, Bethurum was told, had no disease, crime, or politicians.

ABOARD A FLYING SAUCER

Truman Bethurum claimed he had been taken aboard an alien spaceship. There he met the craft's captain, a beautiful alien named Aura Rhanes who spoke in rhyme. Bethurum supposedly met her romantically a number of times, much to the annoyance of his wife. Bethurum wrote a successful book (left), *Aboard a Flying Saucer* (1954), about his experiences

What do YOU think

The "evidence" given here, like all evidence for UFOs, is anecdotal. As a result, most people believe UFOlogy is not a "true" science since it is based on unproven stories and hearsay. Today, much of our interest in the stories does not lie in whether or not they are true. Instead, many people wonder why, in the 1950s, people were so quick to believe these deceptions. They wonder, too, what has changed in our society to make us less likely to believe such stories.

AN ALIEN IN NEW JERSEY

Howard Menger was born in 1922 and says he first saw "space people" as a child. He also claimed to have had many close encounters while in the U.S. Army. In his book *From Outer Space to You* (1959), he wrote about meeting Venusians, some over five hundred years old. They included a number of beautiful women in transparent ski-suits—although the spacewoman in this photograph (above) seems to be wearing a more conventional spacesuit. Menger claims to have helped the Venusians fit into Earthly society. Menger said his second wife Marla was from Venus. In the 1960s, Menger claimed the Central Intelligence Agency (CIA) had asked him to make up the encounters, so they could test public reaction to UFO stories. He also claims men in black (see page 22) tried to prevent him talking about his sightings.

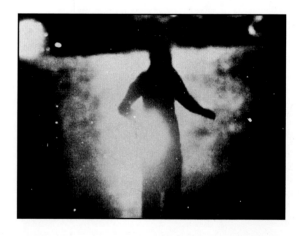

TAKE ME TO YOUR LEADER!

In a close encounter of the fifth kind (CE5) aliens and humans interact. The 1950s appeared to be a great age of interaction between humans and aliens. Many books were published on reported CE5s, and in public lectures, a number of UFOlogists described meetings with space beings. Today, many UFOlogists are embarrassed by these stories. They believe the stories tend to discredit genuine UFO research.

FLYING SAUCERS HAVE LANDED

George Adamski was a waiter who later gave himself the title "professor." Adamski wrote a fictional book about meeting a man from Venus. When he could not find a publisher for the book, he revised the book and presented it as fact rather than fiction. His book *Flying Saucers Have Landed* (1953) became a bestseller (below).

PANCAKES PLEASE

One strange case of a CE5 was reported by Joe Simonton, a sixty-year-old chicken farmer from Wisconsin. In 1961, Simonton claimed he was visited by small, dark-skinned spacemen wearing black suits and balaclavas, or knitted caps that cover the head and shoulders. The aliens asked him for a jug of water, and, in return, they supposedly gave him some pancakes. Simonton ate one of the pancakes, which tasted like cardboard, and sent the others for analysis. They reportedly were made out of ordinary flour but contained no salt. Local people said Simonton was a quiet, ordinary man who normally did not make up amazing stories.

Flying Saucers Have Landed

Desmond Leslie & George Adamski

BEAUTIFUL VENUSIANS

In 1953, George Adamski (right) reportedly saw a UFO in the California desert and went to investigate. He claimed he then met a handsome, sun-tanned young Venusian with long, sandy-colored hair. The Venusian supposedly told him—using hand signs and telepathy— that Venus was Earth's sister planet. The Venusians had come to warn humanity that nuclear radiation could ruin Earth. Adamski later claimed that his Venusian friends took him to Mars, Saturn, and Jupiter.

What do YOU think ❓

Many people do not believe alien
abductions have ever happened. Some
people believe so-called abduction
experiences are a form of mental
delusion. The cases of the Hills
(page 18) and Walton (page 19)
show how television can influence our
subconscious minds. People also have
been observed while having a supposed
abduction experience. In one case
in Australia, two people watched as
someone—who never left their sight—
"met" aliens and "went into" a
spaceship. All the two witnesses saw
was the abductee's physical responses
to what he seemed to be experiencing.
The event may have been a "real" event
inside the head of the abductee, but
the witnesses did not see any aliens.
Even under hypnosis, it is possible to
be fooled. Hypnotists can "suggest"
UFO ideas to a supposed abductee
while the abductee is hypnotized. In
fact, experiments have been done in
which subjects were able to invent
realistic "imaginary abductions" under
hypnosis. Another clue that abduction
"memories" may be false is that most of
them are similar. They involve tunnels,
lights, being covered in liquid, having
difficulty breathing, pain in the navel,
being medically examined, and more.
Women abductees remember having
eggs taken from their ovaries or even
being implanted with alien fetuses. In
these details, most "abductions" seem
more like a flashback to the experience
of being born rather than to the
experience of an alien encounter.

ABDUCTION CASEBOOK

A recent U.S. survey suggests that many people believe they have been abducted by aliens. Some victims reportedly realize they have been abducted only after their memories are drawn out through regression therapy. In this type of therapy, a therapist hypnotizes a person to help him or her re-live past events. One UFOlogist claims we all have been abducted at one time or another—we just may not remember it!

ALL OF THE FOLLOWING SYMPTOMS HAVE BEEN CONSIDERED EVIDENCE OF AN ABDUCTION

- Lost time that reportedly cannot be accounted for
- Scars, bruises, or burns with no memory of what caused them
- Nightmares, especially about aliens, flying, or being eaten by animals with large eyes, such as owls
- Insomnia, especially when caused by the fear of going to sleep
- Medical problems, such as vomiting, headaches, tiredness, or rashes
- Depression
- A UFO sighting; an experience of déjà vu; or a feeling of having second sight, the ability to foresee the future or see events happening elsewhere
- An image repeatedly coming to mind (It may have been put into the brain to block a memory of the abduction.)
- Unaccountable black marks that appear on an X ray of a person's body

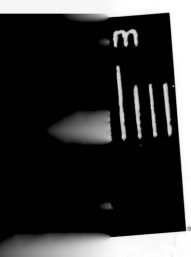

IMPLANTS

Some UFOlogists believe aliens implant tracking devices in the people they abduct, so the aliens can locate the people later. An implant (left) was found in the roof of a supposed abductee's mouth. James Basel, a 17-year-old supposed abductee, shows his alleged alien implant (above).

CASE STUDY 1: ANTONIO VILLAS BOAS, BRAZIL

Name and Occupation: Antonio Villas Boas, farmer

Date: About October 16, 1957

Location: Francisco de Sales, Brazil

Case Description: The day after he reportedly saw a UFO, Antonio Villas Boas was alone on his tractor, plowing a field. He said three humanoids appeared and dragged him on board an egg-shaped craft. On the craft, he claimed the aliens stripped him of his clothes, covered him in a clear liquid, and took a blood sample from his chin.

Investigator s Notes: Villas Boas claimed he tried to fight off his abductors. Doctors found marks and scars all over his body. He also experienced a sickness and sleepiness that resembled radiation poisoning. He remembered his experience without regression therapy and never changed his story. He also remembered seeing some writing over the craft's door:

Right: **An artist's impression of Villa Boas's alien abductor and the craft that landed in his field.**

CASE STUDY 2: BETTY AND BARNEY HILL, UNITED STATES

Name and Occupation: Betty Hill, retired social worker, and Barney Hill, mail worker

Date: September 19, 1961

Location: New Hampshire, United States

Case Description: On their way home one evening, Betty and Barney claimed they were frightened by a UFO. They later found marks on their bodies and realized they had "lost" two hours. They also experienced nightmares and depression. Under regression hypnosis, they remembered being abducted by creatures with "wrap-around" eyes. The creatures forced Barney to give a sperm sample and inserted a needle into Betty's navel. Betty remembered a "star map" the aliens had shown her and drew a copy of it. From this map, UFOlogists deduced the aliens came from Zeta Reticuli, about 30 light-years from Earth.

Investigator s Notes: Although the Hills's friends describe them as an "ordinary couple," Betty has had many psychic experiences. At one time, she claimed UFOs followed her everywhere. Her psychiatrist believed she was suffering delusions after a frightening experience and that her husband had adopted her anxieties into his own memory. Their abduction also happened shortly after a science-fiction program on television showed aliens with "wrap-around" eyes.

Right: **An artist's impression of Betty and Barney Hill during their encounter with a UFO.**

CASE STUDY 3: TRAVIS WALTON, UNITED STATES

Name and Occupation: Travis Walton, forester

Date: November 5, 1975

Location: Arizona, United States

Case Description: On the night of November 5, 1975, a logging team of seven men reportedly saw a UFO. When one of the men, Travis Walton, went to investigate, a beam of light from the craft struck and paralyzed him. His friends fled, believing he was dead. Five days later, Walton turned up in a nearby town. Under regression hypnosis, he remembered being abducted. He said three tall aliens with large eyes examined him, and they showed him a hangar full of UFOs.

Investigator s Notes: The story seems suspicious for several reasons. A show about the Hills's abduction had appeared on TV just one month before the incident, and, at the time of the incident, the men were behind on their work. They may have needed an excuse for their delay. Travis Walton also was known as a practical joker. Twenty-five years later, however, not one of the seven men changed his story.

Right: Travis Walton wrote a book, and his experience was made into a movie **Fire in the Sky** (1993). In the movie, some of the facts were changed. All of the men made money from their story.

CASE STUDY 4: LINDA NAPOLITANO, UNITED STATES

Name and Occupation: Linda Napolitano, housewife

Date: November 30, 1989

Location: New York, United States

Case Description: In 1989, Linda Napolitano was having hypnosis therapy because she believed she had been abducted by aliens a number of times. During her treatment, she revealed that she believed she had been abducted again. Under hypnosis, Linda reported that she remembered being taken out through the walls of her twelfth-story apartment into a spaceship high above the streets of Manhattan. Aliens reportedly medically examined her and then returned her to her bed.

Investigator s Notes: In 1991, this amazing story was given credence. Two Manhattan police officers, who later claimed to be secret service men, reported that they had seen a woman floating in the sky and being taken into a UFO. Later, another witness also claimed to have seen the event.

Right: An artist's impression of Linda Napolitano's abduction from her Manhattan apartment.

FAKES

ROSWELL REVISITED

This photo of a supposed UFO (above) at Roswell is actually a photo of a small UFOlike object thrown toward the setting Sun.

UFOlogy is a tempting field for frauds—people who deceive others just to make money or become famous. Responsible UFOlogists constantly are working to expose fakes because they believe fraudulent claims of UFOs only add to public and government skepticism. The photographs on these pages show how some people have tried to fool us.

VENUSIAN SCOUT CRAFT

Special effects (FX) technology has improved so much that some past fakes now look ridiculous. This photograph (left) of a "scout craft" taken by George Adamski appears to simply be the effects of some light bulbs shining on a metal lamp stand. What Venusian would be brave enough to set off across the Solar System in this "craft"?

What do YOU think **?**

UFO photographers apparently cannot win. Blurred blobs are rejected because they are too indistinct to prove the existence of a UFO, and brilliant images are dismissed as too "perfect" to be true. Despite the thousands of attempted snapshots, one unquestioned, clear photograph of a UFO has yet to be taken.

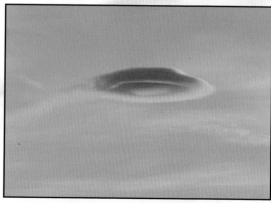

STRANGE CLOUDS OVER HAWAII

Photographed near Hawaii, this so-called UFO (above) is actually a lenticular cloud lit by the rays of the setting Sun.

UFOs OVER NEW YORK

Modern FX technology makes it harder to distinguish fake UFOs from real UFOs.
What is suspicious about this photograph (above) of UFOs over New York City?

ALPINE FAKE

This UFO (left) in the Bernina Mountains is probably just a small model of a spacecraft photographed close up. The spacesuited alien is most likely a toy soldier. The Centro Ufologico Nazionale, Italy's center for UFO studies, exposed the photo as a fake.

What do YOU think ?

HOW TO DETECT A FAKE PHOTOGRAPH

- A photo with no perspective reference to show the size and position of the UFO may be, in reality, just a photo of a small UFO model that was hung up or thrown into the air.
- Variations in the grain of a photo mean that an image has been "pasted" into the photo from somewhere else.
- Irregularities in the angles of lights and shadows between the object and the background show that separate images have been pasted together.
- Differences in color, clarity, or brightness between the UFO and the rest of the photo (as seen at left) are often a sign that the UFO has been painted or stuck on to a pane of glass in front of the camera.
- Bright, luminous blobs or streaks may be spots on the film negative or the camera lens or a reflection on the lens. These effects account for the many UFO pictures people believe are caught by accident.
- Tree branches, telephone lines, or other branching devices above a UFO show that the supposed UFO may be a model hung from the devices.
- Photographs conveniently blurred, fuzzy, or indistinct suggest that the photographer is trying to disguise the fact that the UFO is really a model.

AREA 51, USA

According to the U.S. government, the so-called "Area 51" does not exist as a separate area; it is simply part of a restricted military air base. Many people believe that it may be used for testing new types of military aircraft, such as unmanned aircraft (left). UFO-watchers claim to see crafts regularly performing aerial maneuvers there at night. Some people also believe Area 51 is where the U.S. government has stored the Roswell UFO.

A SECRET TECHNOLOGY

According to Bob Lazar (opposite right), the U.S. government has recovered some crashed UFOs, perhaps resembling this one (opposite left), and is "back-engineering" them; it is examining the technology to see how the crafts work so others can be built.

MEN IN BLACK (MIB)

UFO witnesses sometimes claim to have been followed by "men in black" (MIB) who look like agents of the Federal Bureau of Investigation (FBI). Some UFO-believers say the MIB are actually aliens trying to suppress the truth. Others believe MIB really *are* FBI agents. This MIB (left) is from the movie *Men in Black* (1997).

AREA 51: CONSPIRACY

Some UFO enthusiasts believe the U.S. government knows that aliens exist. They believe the government has worked with aliens for many years, but they believe government workers are secretly agreeing, or conspiring, to say nothing about the aliens. Because these so-called conspiracies are, by definition, a secret, they are hard to disprove. No matter what a government does or says, a conspiracy-theorist believes the government is hiding something. Even when a UFO claim is proven to be a hoax, for example, conspiracy-believers simply claim that the government has misinformed us.

BOB LAZAR

Bob Lazar (above) claims he is an engineer who once worked at Area 51. He says the U.S. government has nine UFOs stored in that area. His testimony often is taken as proof of a government conspiracy— even though there is no proof that Lazar ever worked at Area 51. There also is no proof that he earned an engineering degree from the university he supposedly attended.

TOP SECRET

THE WHITE HOUSE
WASHINGTON D.C.

September 24, 1947

MEMORANDUM FOR THE SECRETARY OF DEFENSE

Dear Secretary Forrestal,

As per our recent conversation on this matter, you are hereby authorized to proceed with all due speed and caution upon your undertaking. Hereafter this matter shall be referred to only as Operation Majestic Twelve.

It continues to be my feeling that any future considerations relative to the ultimate disposition of this matter should rest solely with the Office of the President following appropriate discussions with yourself, Dr. Bush and the Director of Central Intelligence.

Harry Truman

TOP SECRET

MAJESTIC 12

In 1984, a television station received photographs of some documents (left). The documents seemed to prove that, in 1947, the government assigned a group of experts, called the Majestic 12, to study the Roswell UFO. Conspiracy theorists looking at the documents often ignore the fact that they were typed on a typewriter not invented until 1963. The theorists still believe the documents prove the U.S. government has a UFO. They say that if the documents were faked, the government must have faked them in a conscious effort to spread disinformation.

What do YOU think ?

Psychologist Elaine Showalter believes conspiracy theories are deeply damaging to society because they weaken people's faith in institutions such as the government. According to conspiracy theorists, for example, no matter who is elected to an office, no government official can be trusted. Conspiracy theorists encourage others to see the world as a frightening and lonely place.

IS ANYBODY OUT THERE?

The Universe is infinite. Science fiction buffs and UFOlogists believe the Universe is so vast that it cannot possibly be devoid of other lifeforms. They believe that, in the huge expanse of space, the circumstances that led to life on Earth must have occurred elsewhere. Somewhere out there, they reason, hundreds of different kinds of lifeforms of every possible shape, size, and color must exist.

MARS FACE

In 1976, the *Viking* I spacecraft photographed an unusual rock formation on Mars. The 2-mile (3-km)-long formation (above) looked like a face. A collection of pyramid-shaped rocks lay nearby. UFOlogists claimed the formation and rocks were ruins left by an ancient, Egyptianlike civilization. In 1998, however, when the Mars Global Surveyor rephotographed the area, the "Mars Face" looked like a meteor-battered mountain—exactly what it had always been.

BEYOND OUR DREAMS

The Sun, the nearest star to Earth, is 93 million miles (150 million km) away. Given the vast distances aliens would need to travel through space (left), some scientists think it is "unlikely" that aliens have visited our planet. Some people prefer to see UFOs as "paranormal" phenomena. Many UFOlogists, however, find it hard to believe that, in the vastness of space, life is not out there somewhere.

SETI

The Search for Extra-terrestrial Intelligence (SETI) involves searching for radio wave signals possibly sent by other lifeforms in space. The first SETI experiment was held on April 8, 1960. SETI radio telescopes at the Aricebo Observatory in Puerto Rico (right) searched for radio signals from the stars. A regular "whoop, whoop" sound was detected from a star named Epsilon Eridani, but nothing else has since been heard.

LIFE ON MARS

In Antarctica in 1984, a meteorite was discovered that matched the Martian rock studied by the 1976 *Viking* expedition to Mars. Scientists found organic molecules and tiny possible fossils (right). These finds may show that, although life no longer exists on Mars, life *can* develop on other planets.

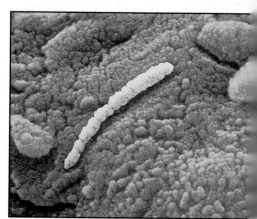

In November 1961, Frank Drake, a U.S. radio astronomer, gave a lecture that changed many people's thinking about whether life exists in outer space. The answer to whether life exists, he said, is in a mathematical equation:

$$N = R^* \times f_p \times n_e \times f_l \times f_i \times f_c \times L.$$

He explained that the number of "space" civilizations (N) is equal to the number of Sun-like stars in the Milky Way (R^*); multiplied by the fraction of those stars that are orbited by planets (f_p), multiplied by the number of those planets able to support life (n_e); multiplied by the fraction of those planets on which life does, by chance, occur (f_l), and evolves intelligence (f_i), and develops an advanced scientific civilization like ours (f_c); multiplied by the number of years that the civilization survives (L).

The problem with this equation is that we don't know the value of any of the factors in it. We can, however, make some reasonable "guesses:"

1. In the Milky Way, about 25 billion stars are roughly similar to our Sun, so $R^* = 25$ billion.

2. Perhaps one in five of these are orbited by planets, so $f_p = \frac{1}{5}$.

3. Perhaps each of those stars has two planets like Earth ($n_e = 2$), and life evolves on one in one hundred ($f_l = \frac{1}{100}$), intelligent life on one in ten of those ($f_i = \frac{1}{10}$), and an advanced civilization comparable to ours exists on one in ten of those ($f_c = \frac{1}{10}$).

4. Perhaps each of those civilizations lasts 1,000 years, in a Universe that has existed at least 10,000 million years, so L = 1,000/10,000 million, or one one-millionth.

Given these "guesses," how many Earthlike civilizations could exist in the Milky Way?

EXTRASOLAR PLANETS

Besides the planets in our Solar System (above), astronomers have discovered other planets in outer space. To find these planets, they study changes they perceive in a star's light to detect "wobbles" in the star's spinning. These wobbles show that another body is orbiting the star. In October 1997, astronomers at a Swiss observatory discovered a planet circling the star 51 Pegasi. The planet is half the size of Jupiter, takes just four days to orbit the star, and has a possible surface temperature of 2,372° F (1,300° C).

ALIEN IMAGES

GENTLE ALIENS

In the television series *Alien Nation* (1989-1990), this actor (above) plays a type of tall, blue-eyed alien. According to the series, this type of alien comes from Sirius, Pleiades, or Venus. It is spiritual, gentle, and loves humans, and its ancestors were the first human beings.

M any UFO enthusiasts believe aliens are among us. Some people even believe aliens have implanted mind-controlling computer chips in some humans. Many beliefs about aliens, however, are fed by science fiction movies and books that create sinister images of aliens. In many of these tales, aliens appear to be indestructible or unharmed by any human technology. Some have acid for blood, others have no feelings, while still others cannot die. The prospect of humans ever being visited by such beings is terrifying. These images fill our imagination. What type of alien would we want to meet on a dark and stormy night?

CHUPACABRAS (GOAT-EATERS)

Chupacabras (above right) are aliens that are said to live in the caves of Puerto Rico. They measure just over 3 feet (1 meter) tall and have huge red eyes, fangs, long claws, and vampirelike wings. They supposedly come out at night to mutilate, kill, and eat livestock. Some UFOlogists believe they are the crew of a crashed spaceship. Others believe they may be creatures that escaped into the jungle when a hurricane destroyed a secret government research installation.

What do YOU think ?

SETI scientists have sent radio messages into space, and the 1977 *Voyager* space probe carried this message: "Greetings. We step out into the Universe seeking only peaceful contact." Some people believe aliens are dangerous, and these messages may just as well say: "Please come and eat us!" UFOlogists do not claim all aliens are dangerous, but many UFOlogists believe aliens are dangerous enough to avoid. According to some abduction stories, however, aliens seem relatively harmless. A common feature of some supposed abductions is that aliens take small, meaningless objects from humans. In one story, aliens stole a bunch of flowers from a woman. In another, they took fishing flies and money. It seems that an attractive trinket is enough to distract aliens and allow a person to escape.

MERRY MARTIANS

Like these Martians (above) from the film *The Man in the Moon* (1960), aliens may be from a highly developed civilization. They may be loving and lovable and change our world to a world of health and happiness.

THE GREYS

The "Grey" (right) is a type of alien that appears in many abduction stories. According to stories about these aliens, they are about 4.5 feet (1.4 m) tall with large heads, huge "wrap-around" eyes, and small bodies. They often are said to come from Andromeda or Zeta Reticuli. Some people say they have a totalitarian society. They supposedly want to conquer Earth and make humans their slaves. Greys also are said to have no feelings, and they conduct medical experiments on humans without using anesthetics.

THE WORLD'S MYSTERIES EXPLORED

FATE

JANUARY 1978 75¢

DEATH BY
HELL'S FIRE

CLOSE
ENCOUNTERS
OF THE
THIRD KIND

REPORT A UFO
AT YOUR OWN RISK

. . .Plus Many Other
Intriguing Features

GREEN-SKINNED MONSTERS

According to some UFO reports (above), UFOs can "turn off" human technology and shoot down military planes. They have paralyzing laser beams and can abduct whole regiments of humans. If these UFOs exist, the aliens piloting them are far more advanced than we are, and they apparently are dangerous.

SHARING THE MESSAGE

In many abduction stories, aliens reportedly want to send an important message to humans. Some aliens are said to report that humans are on a path to self-destruction. They warn of the dangers of nuclear weapons and environmental pollution. Others supposedly give us messages about their technology. In the 1950s, Howard Menger claimed aliens gave him some potatoes from the Moon and a model of the engine that powered their spacecraft (right). None of these reported "messages," however, are particularly new or unknown. Many people question why aliens would travel across the Universe to tell us something we already know. And, having traveled trillions of miles, why would they give the important message to an average citizen and not to the leader of a powerful nation?

GLOBAL CONQUEST

The attempted conquest of Earth by aliens is a favorite theme of science fiction movies, including *Independence Day* (1996) (left). Some UFO enthusiasts genuinely believe aliens are on Earth right now preparing for an invasion. They are supposedly getting ready for Earth's conquest by spreading new diseases and interfering with our weather. Some people question, however, why aliens with the technology to cross the Universe are apparently taking so long to conquer Earth. With their supposed advanced technology, they should need little preparation.

DESPERATE FOR DNA

Some UFO-watchers think aliens are sterile and cannot reproduce, so they need humans to help continue their species. Others believe aliens are genetically mutated in some way, and they are seeking to restore their health by using DNA (left) from humans. Many people question, however, why aliens with such advanced technology would need to abduct so many humans for their experiments.

WHY ARE THEY HERE?

One problem in reports of alien visitors is that the reports do not explain how the aliens reach Earth. One respected UFOlogist thinks alien civilizations exist in the galaxy, but the nearest civilization is 2,000 light-years away. How can aliens travel that huge distance? In science fiction, aliens and humans appear to be able to "fold" space—to travel quickly through it and reconstruct themselves instantly at a new location. In reality, this type of travel seems completely impossible. Some people suggest aliens can travel at the speed of light. For travelers at the speed of light, however, time comes to a standstill. In the time it takes to think, "I must stop now," a person could travel an infinite distance in, for the rest of us, an infinite amount of time. The person would end up beyond the Universe at a time when everyone has long since died. All in all, given the difficulty of getting here, why should aliens want to visit Earth? What do we have that they could possibly want? Theories abound.

SCIENTIFIC EXPERIMENTS

Some UFO enthusiasts believe humans are just a huge genetic experiment that aliens have produced. They believe that, because aliens have no emotions, they want to study human feelings, such as love, fear, and pain. This cover picture from a 1935 magazine (above) shows that these ideas have a long history.

INTERGALACTIC TOURISM

In the movie *Morons from Outer Space* (1985), a group of extraterrestrial "tourists" (left) get lost and literally bump into Earth. Perhaps, as this movie suggests, Earth is just some sort of tourist destination—a galactic "wildlife sanctuary" run by aliens. Alien rangers occasionally come to check that the human "animals" in the sanctuary are healthy, and visiting alien tourists are supposed to stay out of sight. Perhaps we reportedly meet them when these tourists become too curious or forget to stay invisible.

What do YOU think

The many theories about exactly why aliens visit Earth seem to have one common problem. Aliens must have very advanced technology to travel across the Universe and reach Earth, but, according to the theories, aliens do not seem to make much progress once they arrive. Whether they come as scientific observers, conquerors, or do-gooders with a message, they all are still working on achieving their goals— after one hundred years or more of reported alien visits.

TIME SLIP

Occasionally, radio waves seem to "wobble," and listeners find their radio program interrupted briefly by a program on a completely different station. This "wobble" also may happen with the idea of time. We might imagine time as a knife-edge rushing along with a void in front of it and behind it. If time, however, were like a radio signal that sometimes can wobble, then UFOs actually might be random glimpses of a future time. Such time "slips" also could reveal past times and explain other phenomena such as sightings of the Loch Ness monster, ghosts, or the "walking dead." They also could explain déjà vu, the odd feeling that some on-going event has happened before.

THEORIES

Some UFOlogists think the common definition of an alien as an extraterrestrial (ET), or a being originating outside Earth, is misleading. Today, many UFOlogists believe it is unlikely that beings from other galaxies are visiting Earth. They believe UFO experiences are real phenomena, but they seek explanations that do not involve little green men in spaceships. Instead, they define an alien as "something outside normal human experience." Perhaps, some people say, aliens are a type of spiritual manifestation. Richard Miller, a 1950s contactee, claimed an alien from Alpha Centauri told him UFOs were angels. George King, who supposedly was contacted by aliens in 1954, claimed Jesus Christ was an alien from Venus. Other people believe UFOs are demons.

OTHER DIMENSIONS

UFO experiences may be the result of our three-dimensional world coming into contact with other worlds that have either more or fewer dimensions. A creature living in a two-dimensional world would have a form like a sheet of paper; it would have no height, only length and width. Such a creature would not be able to see "up" or "down" because "up" and "down" would not exist in its two-dimensional world. It would only be aware of a very thin slice of the Universe. Now imagine if a ball passed through this creature's world. Until the ball traveled through its world, the creature would be unaware of the ball (above). When the ball did pass through, the creature would see the ball as a mysterious circular shape, growing in diameter, then getting smaller again and finally disappearing as the ball finished passing through. If Earth shares space with and occasionally overlaps worlds having other dimensions, then glimpses of these worlds would be just as fleeting and puzzling for us.

THE "OZ" FACTOR

A still and eerie quiet, known as the "Oz" factor, often is reported to occur just prior to an alien encounter. UFOlogist Jenny Randles sees a similarity between this "Oz" factor and paranormal phenomena such as extra-sensory perception (ESP), out-of-body, or near-death experiences (above). She suggests other beings in the Universe may be trying to get in touch with humans on a psychic level.

What do YOU think

The theories here do not treat UFOlogy as a science but rather as a matter of faith. People cannot prove UFOs exist, and, because the existence of UFOs cannot be proven, believing that they exist must be done on faith.

WAKING DREAMS

Hallucinations, or "waking dreams," can be so vivid that, in a person's memory, what was a hallucination and what was reality may not always be clear. Hallucinations can be disorienting and terrifying. To come to terms with them, the brain might assign the hallucination a concrete and explainable reality. In the past, the brain may have blamed ghosts or demons for the hallucinations. Today, however, because science fiction images and sophisticated technology are familiar to us, our brains may attribute such experiences to aliens (left).

WHY ARE WE SO INTERESTED?

According to Buddhist beliefs, the Buddha (above) was once a prince who lived in a palace and never saw the real world. One day, he left the palace, and, when he saw the suffering happening in the world, he was so horrified that he never returned to the the palace. Today, unlike the Buddha, some people want to "go back to the palace"—to get away from a miserable reality and escape into a fantasy world of aliens and UFOs.

In 1960, two French writers, Jacques Bergier and Louis Pauwels, published *The Morning of the Magicians*, a book that argued that science did not have all the answers. Society, they said, was like a car speeding down a road. It was moving forward, but it was not paying attention to any of the fields and villages along the road. By speeding down the science and technology "road," the authors suggested, humankind was missing, or passing by, many of the important truths about life—truths not explained by science. The book revived interest in experiences that could not be scientifically explained. Perhaps part of the reason people are so interested in reports of UFOs is that UFO phenomena remain a mystery, despite the many theories about them.

ESCAPISM

What do YOU think

People's interest in UFOs and stories about alien encounters will probably never go away. People often are fascinated by the unknown and the frightening. Perhaps some people need the idea of an external threat—such as sinister aliens—to help create a bond between themselves and others. In the end, the existence of extraterrestrial UFOs can never be disproved because science can prove only that something *does* exist, not that something does *not* exist.

THE MARTIANS ARE COMING!

In 1938, a radio play based on the book *The War of the Worlds* (1898) by H. G. Wells was so realistic that it created panic when it was broadcast. The play included fictional news reports of Martians landing on Earth in Grover's Mill, New Jersey. Despite regular announcements that the play was fictional, William Dock (right), 76, of Grover's Mill was ready with a shotgun to ward off the Martian invaders.

THE RISE OF SCI-FI

Authors began to write science fiction (left), or sci-fi, in the late nineteenth century. At that time, many people thought humans would eventually accomplish almost anything through the use of science. Readers found sci-fi fascinating, frightening, and exciting. Today, sci-fi television programs and movies continue to draw fans.

THE SEARCH FOR SOMETHING BEYOND OURSELVES

Humans' psychological need for something larger than themselves to exist somewhere "out there" is as old as humankind itself (above). This need has led to an interest in magic and the supernatural, as well as in the existence of beings from worlds beyond our own.

A SUBCONSCIOUS IMAGE

In his book *Flying Saucers: A Modern Myth* (1958), the great psychologist Carl Jung (right) called UFOs a "rumor." He said UFOs appeal to our subconscious minds—even their circular shape is a powerful subconscious image—and embody our deepest hopes and fears that science and technology will either save or destroy us. He concluded that the fascination with UFOs is a natural and inevitable function of human psychology.

After a UFO sighting, delicate cobweblike material called "angel hair" is sometimes found at the site. An "angel" is also the term given to a false image on a radar screen—an image that may at first be thought to be a UFO.

Some UFOlogists believe UFOs are actually yet-to-be-discovered translucent creatures that live in the sky.

Some people who claim to have been abducted report seeing an alien that looks like an intelligent baby and is a hybrid, or mix, of a human and an alien.

One U.S. government study of unexplained aerial phenomena was called "Project Twinkle." The project had only one camera and failed to photograph a single UFO.

Some people claim they can "channel" the voices of aliens through their own bodies, like a medium supposedly "channels" the voices of the dead.

A "wave" is a number of UFO sightings reported all over the world in quick succession. A "hot spot" is a place where UFOs are often "seen."

Some people claim to be able to use supernatural powers to "see" events or objects that are far away. Sometimes, they "see" UFOs.

The government of the former Soviet Union took UFOs very seriously and organized a series of investigations. Now, Russia has an area similar to Area 51. The area, known as the "M-zone," is in the Ural Mountains.

One UFOlogist claims that UFOs move by creating special electrical and gravitational fields. By varying the strength of the fields, the UFOs can move at great speeds.

FOR FURTHER INFORMATION

WEB SITES

Unsolved Mysteries **www.kyrene.k12.az.us/schools/brisas/sunda/mystery/**

SETI Institute **www.seti.org**

NASA Kids **http://kids.msfc.nasa.gov/**

BOOKS

Asimov, Isaac and Richard Hantula. UFOs. Isaac Asimov's 21st Century Library of the Universe series (Gareth Stevens)

Perry, Janet and Victor Gentle. *Aliens*. Monsters series (Gareth Stevens)

Twist, Clint. *The Search for Life in Space*. Science Quest series (Gareth Stevens)

abduction—the act of taking a person away by force. The person taken is called an **abductee**

anecdotal—relating to a short, often entertaining, story of an incident or event that usually happened in the life of the person telling the story

autokinesis—a visual illusion that a stationary light source is moving. It occurs after staring for a long time at a small, dim, fixed light source in a dark room or outside on a dark night

black hole—an object in the Solar System with a gravitational field so strong that light cannot escape it

conspiracy—an agreement between two or more people to secretly perform an unlawful or evil act

déjà vu—the feeling that one has experienced a scene or event before when one actually is experiencing it for the first time

devoid—without, or lacking

discredit—to destroy or injure the credibility of or confidence in a person, theory, or institution

Geiger counters—instruments used to detect radioactivity

genes—tiny parts of animals or plants that determine what characteristics the animals or plants will have and what they will pass on to offspring

hoaxers—people who try to deceive or trick others, often into believing that something fake is actually genuine

hypnosis—a trancelike state characterized by a readiness to respond to suggestions. This state resembles sleep and is artificially

induced in one peron by another person

impervious—not allowing anything to pierce, enter, or otherwise penetrate

lenticular cloud—a lens-shaped cloud, often formed as a result of winds passing over mountains

light-year—a unit of measurement equal to the distance light travels in one year; approximately 5.88 trillion miles (9.46 trillion km)

medieval—relating to the Middle Ages, a time in European history that stretches from about 500 to 1500

meteor—a piece of matter from space that burns up as it enters Earth's atmosphere. **Meteorites** are meteors that reach Earth's surface before burning up completely

mutated—changed or altered

mutilate—injure or disfigure, usually by cutting off a limb or other parts

paranormal—unable to be explained by scientific reasons

phenomenon (*pl.* phenomena)—an act or an object perceived by the senses; a rare event

psychic—outside the area of natural or scientific knowledge, often nonphysical or spiritual in force

seismographs—instruments used for recording the vibrations of an earthquake

translucent—permitting light to pass through

wildlife sanctuary—a place where animals can live protected from hunters